Games

For a free color catalog describing Gareth Stevens' list of high-quality books, call 1-800-542-2595 (USA) or 1-800-461-9120 (Canada). Gareth Stevens' Fax: (414) 225-0377.

Library of Congress Cataloging-in-Publication Data

Griffiths, Rose.
    Games/by Rose Griffiths; photographs by Peter Millard.
        p. cm. -- (First step math)
    Originally published: London: A&C Black, 1993, in series:
Simple maths.
    Includes bibliographical references and index.
    ISBN 0-8368-1111-9
    1. Mathematics--Study and teaching (Elementary). 2. Games in
mathematics education. [1. Games. 2. Mathematical recreations.]
I. Millard, Peter, ill. II. Title. III. Series.
QA135.5.G693   1994
793'.01'51--dc20   94-10038

This edition first published in 1994 by
Gareth Stevens Publishing
1555 North RiverCenter Drive, Suite 201
Milwaukee, Wisconsin 53212, USA

Series editor: Patricia Lantier-Sampon
Editorial assistants: Mary Dykstra, Diane Laska
Mathematics consultant: Mike Spooner

Printed in the United States of America
1 2 3 4 5 6 7 8 9 99 98 97 96 95 94

At this time, Gareth Stevens, Inc., does not use 100 percent recycled paper, although the paper used in our books does contain about 30 percent recycled fiber. This decision was made after a careful study of current recycling procedures revealed their dubious environmental benefits. We will continue to explore recycling options.

Games

by Rose Griffiths
photographs by Peter Millard

Gareth Stevens Publishing
MILWAUKEE

Do you know how to play
these games?

Where shall I put
the game piece?

5

We can play lots of different card games.

7

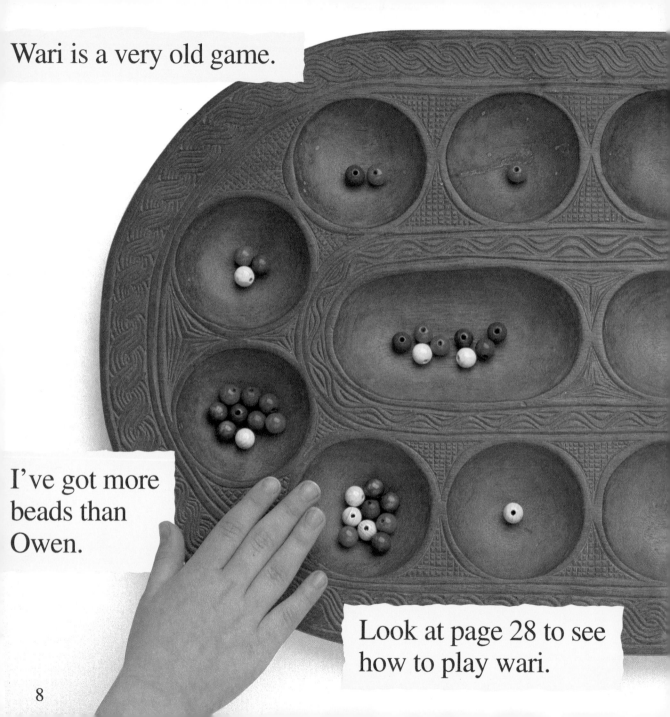

Wari is a very old game.

I've got more beads than Owen.

Look at page 28 to see how to play wari.

8

Computer games are fun.

What's your favorite
computer game?

9

We've just made up this game.

How do you think we play it?

How many animals will the farmer catch?

Owen drew this track
for a racing game.

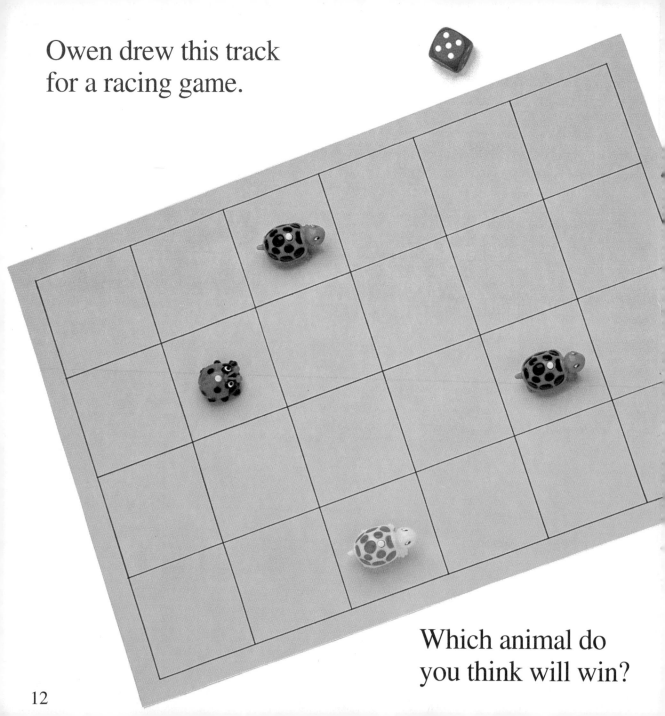

Which animal do
you think will win?

12

Owen changes the rules sometimes.

Will the people catch the chickens?

We've made
some snakes
and ladders.

Where shall I put
this snake?

14

Where does this number go?

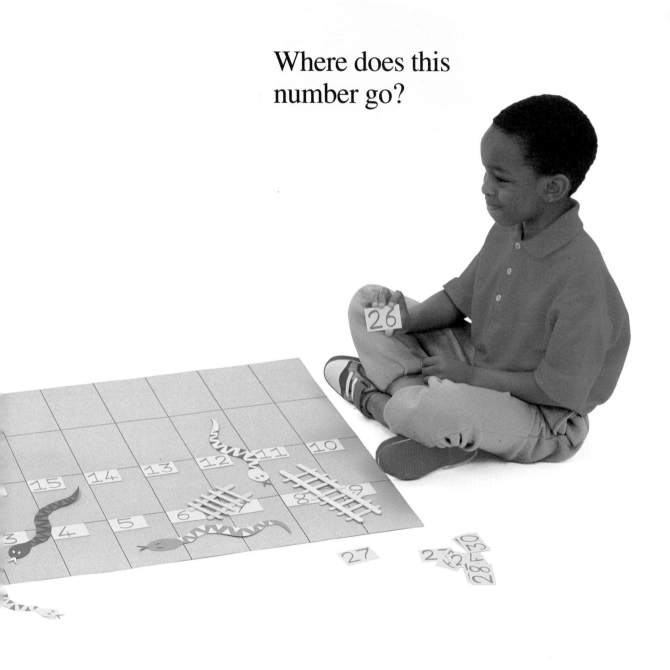

If I practice this
game, I get better
at playing it.

16

But some games just
depend on luck.

Heads to move
the green car.
Tails to
move the
yellow car.

Dominoes depends on luck and skill.

18

I'm playing a memory game.

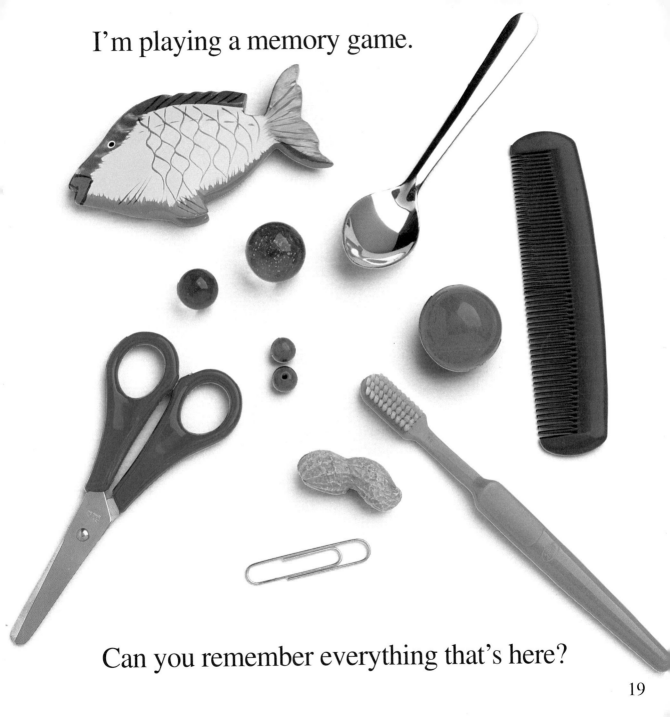

Can you remember everything that's here?

What have I taken away?

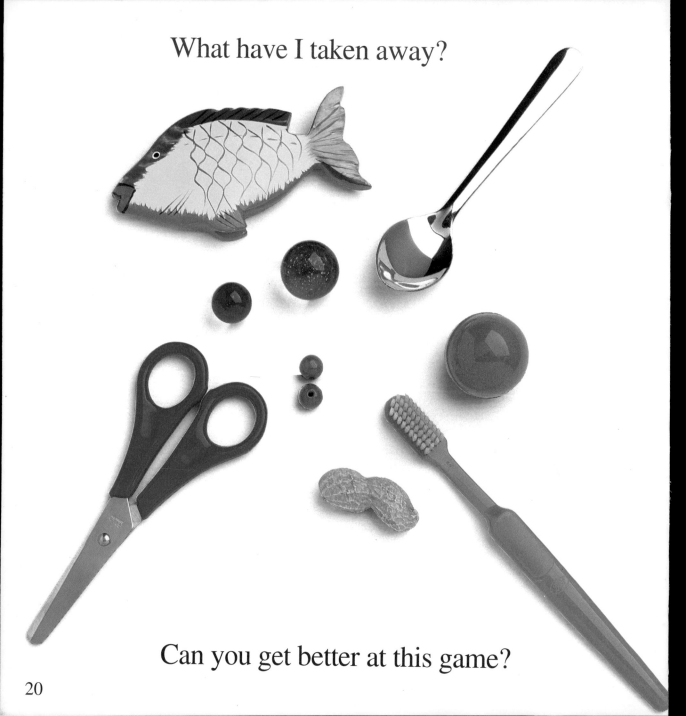

Can you get better at this game?

I'll try to be first to match all the pictures on my card.

Does this game need luck or skill?

We're playing a stepping game.

If the spinner stops on red, Owen moves.

If it stops on blue, Alice moves.

Do we both have
the same chance
of winning?

We like playing soccer.

Which games do you like playing?

25

FOR MORE INFORMATION

Notes for Parents and Teachers

As you share this book with young readers, these notes may help you explain the mathematical principles behind the different activities.

pages 4, 5, 6, 7, 8, 11, 13, 17, 22, 23
Games have rules

Explaining and discussing the rules of a simple game require children to think logically and to consider alternative ways of explaining things. Sometimes, as with cards and dominoes, the same game pieces can be used, with different rules, to play several different games. People can alter games if they wish, but they should agree on the rules they will use before playing.

pages 8, 9
Old and new games

The game of wari (also called ayo, songe, congklak, or mancala) has been played all over the world for hundreds of years. It is particularly popular in Africa and Southeast Asia. Wari gives children practice in counting and thinking ahead. The rules of wari vary from one country to another. Computer games are a relatively new invention. Like other games, they vary a great deal in how mathematically useful they are.

pages 10, 11, 12, 13, 14, 15, 17
Inventing games

Making and playing games can help children practice many mathematical skills, such as estimating, measuring, counting, matching, sorting, and using shapes. Children whose skills of measuring and drawing are still at an early stage may need an adult to draw simple tracks or boards for them. This leaves the children free to experiment with movable components until they are happy with the games they invent.

pages 16, 17, 18, 19, 20, 21, 23
Luck or skill?

Ideas about luck take a long time to develop. For example, children may think they can learn to throw dice to get a particular number when they want it or that wishing hard will help. Playing the same dice game several times and discussing the results may help children arrive at more realistic conclusions. Many children can also learn about strategies and tactics if they act as a "helper" to an older child or an adult player.

pages 22, 23
Fair or unfair?

It's a good idea to let children try the "stepping game" for themselves. Since the spinner has four blue sections and only two red ones, the child in the blue shirt is twice as likely to win. Playing a game like this helps children think about probability.

pages 24, 25 Surveys

Children may enjoy carrying out a survey of favorite games. See how many different ways of sorting and classifying games they can think of. Some possible categories might be: games of skill or chance, competitive or cooperative games, and indoor or outdoor games.

Things to Do

1. Create a game
Use your imagination to design your own game, perhaps like the snakes and ladders shown in this book. Will your game depend on skill or luck? How many players can play your new game? What will be your game rules? What will you call your game?

2. Play wari
Collect forty-eight beans, beads, or smooth stones and make a playing board from an egg carton (cut the carton lengthwise in half, so there will be two sets of six holes) and two small margarine tubs. The two players each have a row of six holes (carton) and one tub. The tub is used to store beads collected during the game. Set the cartons and tubs up in a way that is somewhat similar to the wari game pictured on pages 8-9. Here is one way to play:
To start, put four beads in each of the twelve holes. When it is your turn, pick up all the beads in one of the six holes on your side. Then put the beads, one in each hole, in the next few holes going counterclockwise around the board. If the last hole you put a bead in now has either two or three beads in it — and is not on your side — you can put the beads in your store (tub). You can also keep the beads from the hole before the last one if this has two or three beads in it. But if you take the other player's last beads, you lose the game! The game stops when one player has no beads left. If you have the most beads in your tub, you win the wari game.

Fun Facts about Games

1. In some parts of Africa, children play wari and other games on "playing boards" scooped out of the ground.

2. Dominoes can be traced back to China, perhaps as early as the twelfth century.

3. The first dominoes were made of thin pieces of bone. Later on, they were made from wood and then plastic.

4. The word *hopscotch* comes from an old word meaning "to mark lightly." If you play hopscotch, you may mark the sidewalk lightly with chalk.

5. The numbers on the opposite sides of a die always add up to seven. Dice probably originated in Asia. They have been found in Egyptian tombs and are mentioned in ancient Greek and Roman literature.

6. Chinese checkers is a modern version of the game of Halma (from the Greek word meaning "a leap"), which was invented in England about 1880.

7. Most scholars agree that the game of chess originated in the Indus Valley of India in about the seventh century, perhaps from another, similar game called chaturanga (the "army game"). The game pieces used in modern games of chess, however, date back to approximately the fifteenth century, when they gained their present form.

Glossary

change — to alter or make different.

depend — to rely on something or someone for information, help, protection, or support.

dominoes — a game played with wooden or plastic rectangular tiles in which players match the number of dots on the playing pieces.

games — activities for amusement or play. Games usually have sets of rules to ensure fair play.

heads — the top side or face of a coin, the opposite of *tails*.

practice — to do something over and over again in order to improve skills.

rules — instructions for playing a game. Rules help players know what they may and may not do to play the game fairly.

skill — the ability to do something well. Although some games may seem confusing and difficult at first, players can often improve their skill by playing the game over and over again.

solitaire — a card game that can be played alone. In England, solitaire is called patience.

tails — the bottom side of a coin, the opposite of *heads*.

track — a course for racing or moving upon in a game.

wari — a game in which players use beads, seeds, beans, or other markers to play.

Places to Visit

Everything we do involves some basic mathematical principles. Listed below are a few museums that offer a variety of mathematical information and experiences. You may also be able to locate other museums in your area. Just remember: you don't always have to visit a museum to experience the wonders of mathematics. Math is everywhere!

The Smithsonian Institution
1000 Jefferson Drive SW
Washington, D.C. 20560

Ontario Science Center
770 Don Mills Road
Don Mills, Ontario
M3C 1T3

Royal British Columbia Museum
675 Belleview Street
Victoria, British Columbia
V8V 1X4

Museum of Science and Industry
57th Street and Lake Shore Drive
Chicago, IL 60637

More Books to Read

*The Book of Classic
    Board Games*
    John Cassidy
    (Klutz Press)

*Games: Some Old, Some New,
    All Fun to Do*
    Imogene Forte
    (Incentive Publishing)

Games of the World
Frederic Grunfeld
(Ballantine Books)

*Great Games to Play
with Groups*
Frank Harris
(Fearon Publishers)

*Kate Greenaway's Book
of Games*
Kate Greenaway
(St. Martin's Press)

My First Gamebook
Katy Dobbs
(Workman Publishing)

Videotapes

Play Along Games and Songs
(My Sesame Street Videos)

Sports and Games
(Tell Me Why Videos)

Index